CHICKEN TRACKER'S JOURNAL:

KEEPING IT ALL TOGETHER

By Kjasen

Chicken Tracker's Journal: Keeping It All Together

April 2016

Illustrations from Pixabay.com

ISBN-13: 978-0692703410

To all the chickens
& chicken lovers in the world!

CHICKEN'S HOME PAGE:

Page #___ ______________________________

Page #___ ______________________________

Page #___ ______________________________

Page #___ ______________________________

Page #___ ______________________________

Page #___ ______________________________

Page #___ ______________________________

Page #___ ______________________________

Page #___ ______________________________

Page #___ ______________________________

Page #___ ______________________________

Page #___ ______________________________

My Chicken's Home

(Place photo or sketch here)

CHICKEN # 1

Chicken's Name:______________________________________

☐ Hen ☐ Rooster

Purpose: ☐ Egg-Layer ☐ Meat ☐ Pet ☐ Other __________

Chicken's Breed: ______________________________________

Colors/Identifying Marks:_________________________________

____

Date Acquired: ____

Approx. Age/Hatch Date: ________________________________

Diet/Feed____

____

Place Chicken's Photo Here

HEALTH RECORD: (Healthy or Ill)

Date ________________ Condition/Illness ____________________________

____

Treatment (if needed): ____

____

____

HEALTH RECORD: (Healthy or Ill)

Date ________________ Condition/Illness ____________________________

____

Treatment (if needed): ____

____

____

HEALTH RECORD: (Healthy or Ill)

Date ________________ Condition/Illness ____________________________

____

Treatment (if needed): ____

____

____

HEALTH RECORD: (Healthy or Ill)

Date ________________ Condition/Illness ____________________________

____

Treatment (if needed): ____

____

____

HEALTH RECORD: (Healthy or Ill)

Date ________________ Condition/Illness ____________________________

____

Treatment (if needed): ____

____

____

HEALTH RECORD: (Healthy or Ill)

Date ________________ Condition/Illness ____________________________

____

Treatment (if needed): ____

____

____

NOTES AND OBSERVATIONS:

NOTES AND OBSERVATIONS:

NOTES AND OBSERVATIONS:

PHOTOS AND SKETCHES

"If I hadn't started painting, I would have raised chickens."

Grandma Moses

PHOTOS AND SKETCHES

PHOTOS AND SKETCHES

CHICKEN # 2

Chicken's Name:____

☐ Hen ☐ Rooster

Purpose: ☐ Egg-Layer ☐ Meat ☐ Pet ☐ Other __________

Chicken's Breed: ______________________________________

Colors/Identifying Marks:__________________________________

____

Date Acquired: ____

Approx. Age/Hatch Date: _________________________________

Diet/Feed____

____

Place Chicken's Photo Here

HEALTH RECORD: (Healthy or Ill)

Date ________________ Condition/Illness____________________________

____

Treatment (if needed):____

____

____

HEALTH RECORD: (Healthy or Ill)

Date ________________ Condition/Illness____________________________

____

Treatment (if needed):____

____

____

HEALTH RECORD: (Healthy or Ill)

Date ________________ Condition/Illness____________________________

____

Treatment (if needed):____

____

____

HEALTH RECORD: (Healthy or Ill)

Date ________________ Condition/Illness_____________________________

____

Treatment (if needed):____

____

____

HEALTH RECORD: (Healthy or Ill)

Date ________________ Condition/Illness_____________________________

____

Treatment (if needed):____

____

____

HEALTH RECORD: (Healthy or Ill))

Date ________________ Condition/Illness_____________________________

____

Treatment (if needed):____

____

____

NOTES AND OBSERVATIONS:

NOTES AND OBSERVATIONS:

NOTES AND OBSERVATIONS:

PHOTOS AND SKETCHES

PHOTOS AND SKETCHES

PHOTOS AND SKETCHES

"I began raising chickens primarily for their eggs, but over the years, I've also grown fond of caring for them and learning about their many different breeds and varieties." Martha Stewart

CHICKEN # 3

Chicken's Name:____

☐ Hen ☐ Rooster

Purpose: ☐ Egg-Layer ☐ Meat ☐ Pet ☐ Other __________

Chicken's Breed: ____

Colors/Identifying Marks:___________________________________

____

Date Acquired: ____

Approx. Age/Hatch Date: __________________________________

Diet/Feed____

____

Place Chicken's Photo Here

HEALTH RECORD: (Healthy or Ill)

Date ________________ Condition/Illness______________________________

____

Treatment (if needed):____

____

____

HEALTH RECORD: (Healthy or Ill)

Date ________________ Condition/Illness______________________________

____

Treatment (if needed):____

____

____

HEALTH RECORD: (Healthy or Ill)

Date ________________ Condition/Illness______________________________

____

Treatment (if needed):____

____

____

HEALTH RECORD: (Healthy or Ill)

Date ________________ Condition/Illness____________________________

____

Treatment (if needed):____

____

____

HEALTH RECORD: (Healthy or Ill)

Date ________________ Condition/Illness____________________________

____

Treatment (if needed):____

____

____

HEALTH RECORD: (Healthy or Ill)

Date ________________ Condition/Illness____________________________

____

Treatment (if needed):____

____

____

NOTES AND OBSERVATIONS:

NOTES AND OBSERVATIONS:

NOTES AND OBSERVATIONS:

PHOTOS AND SKETCHES

PHOTOS AND SKETCHES

PHOTOS AND SKETCHES

CHICKEN # 4

Chicken's Name:____

☐ Hen ☐ Rooster

Purpose: ☐ Egg-Layer ☐ Meat ☐ Pet ☐ Other __________

Chicken's Breed: ______________________________________

Colors/Identifying Marks:_________________________________

____

Date Acquired: ____

Approx. Age/Hatch Date: _________________________________

Diet/Feed____

____

Place Chicken's Photo Here

HEALTH RECORD: (Healthy or Ill)

Date ________________ Condition/Illness____________________________

____

Treatment (if needed):____

____

____

HEALTH RECORD: (Healthy or Ill)

Date ________________ Condition/Illness____________________________

____

Treatment (if needed):____

____

____

HEALTH RECORD: (Healthy or Ill))

Date ________________ Condition/Illness____________________________

____

Treatment (if needed):____

____

____

HEALTH RECORD: (Healthy or Ill)

Date ________________ Condition/Illness______________________________

____

Treatment (if needed):____

____

____

HEALTH RECORD: (Healthy or Ill)

Date ________________ Condition/Illness______________________________

____

Treatment (if needed):____

____

____

HEALTH RECORD: (Healthy or Ill))

Date ________________ Condition/Illness______________________________

____

Treatment (if needed):____

____

____

NOTES AND OBSERVATIONS:

NOTES AND OBSERVATIONS:

NOTES AND OBSERVATIONS:

PHOTOS AND SKETCHES

PHOTOS AND SKETCHES

PHOTOS AND SKETCHES

CHICKEN # 5

Chicken's Name:____________________________________

☐ Hen ☐ Rooster

Purpose: ☐ Egg-Layer ☐ Meat ☐ Pet ☐ Other __________

Chicken's Breed: ____________________________________

Colors/Identifying Marks:______________________________

____

Date Acquired: ______________________________________

Approx. Age/Hatch Date: ______________________________

Diet/Feed____

____

Place Chicken's Photo Here

HEALTH RECORD: (Healthy or Ill)

Date ________________ Condition/Illness____________________________

____

Treatment (if needed):____

____

____

HEALTH RECORD: (Healthy or Ill)

Date ________________ Condition/Illness____________________________

____

Treatment (if needed):____

____

____

HEALTH RECORD: (Healthy or Ill))

Date ________________ Condition/Illness____________________________

____

Treatment (if needed):____

____

____

HEALTH RECORD: (Healthy or Ill)

Date ________________ Condition/Illness_____________________________

____

Treatment (if needed):____

____

____

HEALTH RECORD: (Healthy or Ill)

Date ________________ Condition/Illness_____________________________

____

Treatment (if needed):____

____

____

HEALTH RECORD: (Healthy or Ill))

Date ________________ Condition/Illness_____________________________

____

Treatment (if needed):____

____

____

NOTES AND OBSERVATIONS:

NOTES AND OBSERVATIONS:

NOTES AND OBSERVATIONS:

PHOTOS AND SKETCHES

PHOTOS AND SKETCHES

PHOTOS AND SKETCHES

CHICKEN # 6

Chicken's Name:____

☐ Hen ☐ Rooster

Purpose: ☐ Egg-Layer ☐ Meat ☐ Pet ☐ Other ___________

Chicken's Breed: ____

Colors/Identifying Marks:___________________________________

____

Date Acquired: ____

Approx. Age/Hatch Date: __________________________________

Diet/Feed____

____

Place Chicken's Photo Here

HEALTH RECORD: (Healthy or Ill)

Date ________________ Condition/Illness______________________________

____

Treatment (if needed):____

____

____

HEALTH RECORD: (Healthy or Ill)

Date ________________ Condition/Illness______________________________

____

Treatment (if needed):____

____

____

HEALTH RECORD: (Healthy or Ill))

Date ________________ Condition/Illness______________________________

____

Treatment (if needed):____

____

____

HEALTH RECORD: (Healthy or Ill)

Date ________________ Condition/Illness_____________________________

____

Treatment (if needed):____

____

____

HEALTH RECORD: (Healthy or Ill)

Date ________________ Condition/Illness_____________________________

____

Treatment (if needed):____

____

____

HEALTH RECORD: (Healthy or Ill))

Date ________________ Condition/Illness_____________________________

____

Treatment (if needed):____

____

____

NOTES AND OBSERVATIONS:

NOTES AND OBSERVATIONS:

NOTES AND OBSERVATIONS:

PHOTOS AND SKETCHES

"I'm not counting any chickens". Jeff Bridges

PHOTOS AND SKETCHES

PHOTOS AND SKETCHES

CHICKEN # 7

Chicken's Name:____

☐ Hen ☐ Rooster

Purpose: ☐ Egg-Layer ☐ Meat ☐ Pet ☐ Other __________

Chicken's Breed: ____

Colors/Identifying Marks:________________________________

____

Date Acquired: ____

Approx. Age/Hatch Date: __________________________________

Diet/Feed____

____

Place Chicken's Photo Here

HEALTH RECORD: (Healthy or Ill)

Date ________________ Condition/Illness______________________________

____

Treatment (if needed):____

____

____

HEALTH RECORD: (Healthy or Ill)

Date ________________ Condition/Illness______________________________

____

Treatment (if needed):____

____

____

HEALTH RECORD: (Healthy or Ill))

Date ________________ Condition/Illness______________________________

____

Treatment (if needed):____

____

____

HEALTH RECORD: (Healthy or Ill)

Date ________________ Condition/Illness____________________________

____

Treatment (if needed):____

____

____

HEALTH RECORD: (Healthy or Ill)

Date ________________ Condition/Illness____________________________

____

Treatment (if needed):____

____

____

HEALTH RECORD: (Healthy or Ill))

Date ________________ Condition/Illness____________________________

____

Treatment (if needed):____

____

____

NOTES AND OBSERVATIONS:

NOTES AND OBSERVATIONS:

NOTES AND OBSERVATIONS:

PHOTOS AND SKETCHES

PHOTOS AND SKETCHES

PHOTOS AND SKETCHES

CHICKEN # 8

Chicken's Name:____

☐ Hen ☐ Rooster

Purpose: ☐ Egg-Layer ☐ Meat ☐ Pet ☐ Other ___________

Chicken's Breed: ____

Colors/Identifying Marks:___________________________________

____

Date Acquired: ____

Approx. Age/Hatch Date: ___________________________________

Diet/Feed____

____

Place Chicken's Photo Here

HEALTH RECORD: (Healthy or Ill)

Date ________________ Condition/Illness ____________________________

____

Treatment (if needed): ____

____

____

HEALTH RECORD: (Healthy or Ill)

Date ________________ Condition/Illness ____________________________

____

Treatment (if needed): ____

____

____

HEALTH RECORD: (Healthy or Ill))

Date ________________ Condition/Illness ____________________________

____

Treatment (if needed): ____

____

____

HEALTH RECORD: (Healthy or Ill)

Date ________________ Condition/Illness ____________________________

____

Treatment (if needed): ____

____

____

HEALTH RECORD: (Healthy or Ill)

Date ________________ Condition/Illness ____________________________

____

Treatment (if needed): ____

____

____

HEALTH RECORD: (Healthy or Ill))

Date ________________ Condition/Illness ____________________________

____

Treatment (if needed): ____

____

____

NOTES AND OBSERVATIONS:

NOTES AND OBSERVATIONS:

NOTES AND OBSERVATIONS:

PHOTOS AND SKETCHES

PHOTOS AND SKETCHES

PHOTOS AND SKETCHES

CHICKEN # 9

Chicken's Name:____

☐ Hen ☐ Rooster

Purpose: ☐ Egg-Layer ☐ Meat ☐ Pet ☐ Other __________

Chicken's Breed: ____

Colors/Identifying Marks:__________________________________

____

Date Acquired: ____

Approx. Age/Hatch Date: __________________________________

Diet/Feed____

____

Place Chicken's Photo Here

HEALTH RECORD: (Healthy or Ill)

Date ________________ Condition/Illness_____________________________

____

Treatment (if needed):____

____

____

HEALTH RECORD: (Healthy or Ill)

Date ________________ Condition/Illness_____________________________

____

Treatment (if needed):____

____

____

HEALTH RECORD: (Healthy or Ill))

Date ________________ Condition/Illness_____________________________

____

Treatment (if needed):____

____

____

HEALTH RECORD: (Healthy or Ill)

Date ________________ Condition/Illness____________________________

____

Treatment (if needed):____

____

____

HEALTH RECORD: (Healthy or Ill)

Date ________________ Condition/Illness____________________________

____

Treatment (if needed):____

____

____

HEALTH RECORD: (Healthy or Ill))

Date ________________ Condition/Illness____________________________

____

Treatment (if needed):____

____

____

NOTES AND OBSERVATIONS:

NOTES AND OBSERVATIONS:

NOTES AND OBSERVATIONS:

PHOTOS AND SKETCHES

PHOTOS AND SKETCHES

"Chicken see, Chicken do" unknown

PHOTOS AND SKETCHES

CHICKEN # 10

Chicken's Name:____

☐ Hen ☐ Rooster

Purpose: ☐ Egg-Layer ☐ Meat ☐ Pet ☐ Other __________

Chicken's Breed: ____

Colors/Identifying Marks:__________________________________

____

Date Acquired: ____

Approx. Age/Hatch Date: __________________________________

Diet/Feed____

____

Place Chicken's Photo Here

HEALTH RECORD: (Healthy or Ill)

Date ________________ Condition/Illness____________________________

____

Treatment (if needed):____

____

____

HEALTH RECORD: (Healthy or Ill)

Date ________________ Condition/Illness____________________________

____

Treatment (if needed):____

____

____

HEALTH RECORD: (Healthy or Ill))

Date ________________ Condition/Illness____________________________

____

Treatment (if needed):____

____

____

HEALTH RECORD: (Healthy or Ill)

Date ________________ Condition/Illness ______________________________

____

Treatment (if needed): ____

____

____

HEALTH RECORD: (Healthy or Ill)

Date ________________ Condition/Illness ______________________________

____

Treatment (if needed): ____

____

____

HEALTH RECORD: (Healthy or Ill))

Date ________________ Condition/Illness ______________________________

____

Treatment (if needed): ____

____

____

NOTES AND OBSERVATIONS:

NOTES AND OBSERVATIONS:

NOTES AND OBSERVATIONS:

PHOTOS AND SKETCHES

PHOTOS AND SKETCHES

PHOTOS AND SKETCHES

CHICKEN # 11

Chicken's Name:______________________________________

☐ Hen ☐ Rooster

Purpose: ☐ Egg-Layer ☐ Meat ☐ Pet ☐ Other __________

Chicken's Breed: ______________________________________

Colors/Identifying Marks:______________________________

____

Date Acquired: ____

Approx. Age/Hatch Date: _______________________________

Diet/Feed____

____

Place Chicken's Photo Here

HEALTH RECORD: (Healthy or Ill)

Date ________________ Condition/Illness ______________________________

____

Treatment (if needed): ____

____

____

HEALTH RECORD: (Healthy or Ill)

Date ________________ Condition/Illness ______________________________

____

Treatment (if needed): ____

____

____

HEALTH RECORD: (Healthy or Ill))

Date ________________ Condition/Illness ______________________________

____

Treatment (if needed): ____

____

____

HEALTH RECORD: (Healthy or Ill)

Date ________________ Condition/Illness____________________________

____

Treatment (if needed):____

____

____

HEALTH RECORD: (Healthy or Ill)

Date ________________ Condition/Illness____________________________

____

Treatment (if needed):____

____

____

HEALTH RECORD: (Healthy or Ill))

Date ________________ Condition/Illness____________________________

____

Treatment (if needed):____

____

____

NOTES AND OBSERVATIONS:

NOTES AND OBSERVATIONS:

NOTES AND OBSERVATIONS:

PHOTOS AND SKETCHES

PHOTOS AND SKETCHES

PHOTOS AND SKETCHES

CHICKEN # 12

Chicken's Name:____

☐ Hen ☐ Rooster

Purpose: ☐ Egg-Layer ☐ Meat ☐ Pet ☐ Other ___________

Chicken's Breed: ____

Colors/Identifying Marks:__________________________________

____

Date Acquired: ____

Approx. Age/Hatch Date: __________________________________

Diet/Feed____

____

Place Chicken's Photo Here

HEALTH RECORD: (Healthy or Ill)

Date ________________ Condition/Illness_____________________________

____

Treatment (if needed):____

____

____

HEALTH RECORD: (Healthy or Ill)

Date ________________ Condition/Illness_____________________________

____

Treatment (if needed):____

____

____

HEALTH RECORD: (Healthy or Ill))

Date ________________ Condition/Illness_____________________________

____

Treatment (if needed):____

____

____

HEALTH RECORD: (Healthy or Ill)

Date ________________ Condition/Illness ____________________________

____

Treatment (if needed): ____

____

____

HEALTH RECORD: (Healthy or Ill)

Date ________________ Condition/Illness ____________________________

____

Treatment (if needed): ____

____

____

HEALTH RECORD: (Healthy or Ill))

Date ________________ Condition/Illness ____________________________

____

Treatment (if needed): ____

____

____

NOTES AND OBSERVATIONS:

NOTES AND OBSERVATIONS:

NOTES AND OBSERVATIONS:

PHOTOS AND SKETCHES

PHOTOS AND SKETCHES

PHOTOS AND SKETCHES

~GROUP PHOTOS~

~GROUP PHOTOS~

~GROUP PHOTOS~

CPSIA information can be obtained at www.ICGtesting.com
Printed in the USA
LVOW09s1023150616
492711LV00007B/154/P